KW-051-565

2 3 JUN 2025

WITHDRAWN

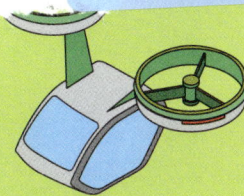

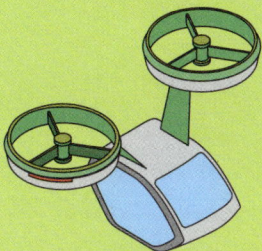

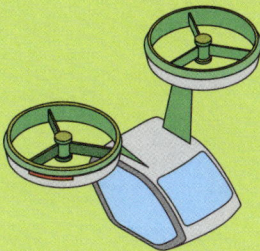

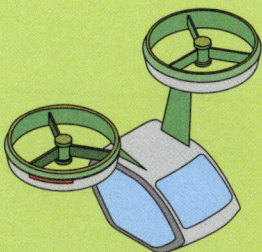

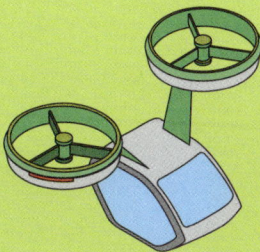

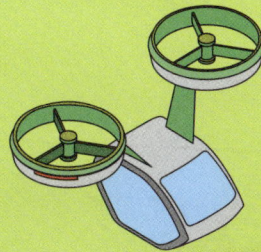

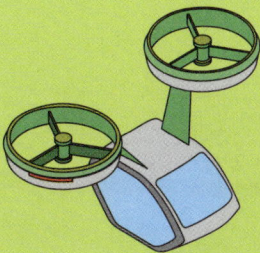

MAKER MODELS

TRANSPORT HUB

Anna Claybourne

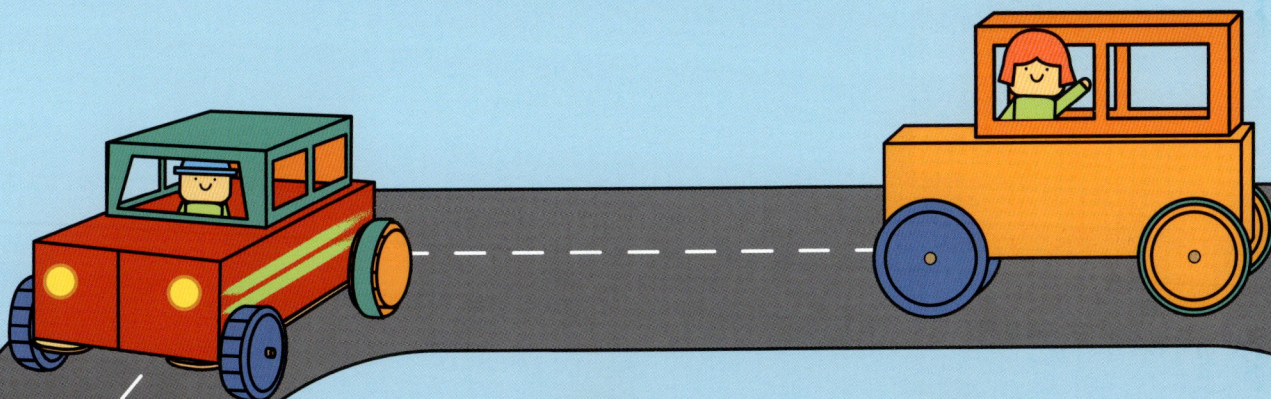

WAYLAND

www.waylandbooks.co.uk

First published in Great Britain in 2019
by Wayland
Copyright © Hodder and Stoughton, 2019
All rights reserved.

Editor: Elise Short
Design and illustration: Collaborate

HB ISBN: 978 1 5263 0747 7
PB ISBN: 978 1 5263 0748 4

Printed and bound in China

MIX
Paper from
responsible sources
FSC® C104740
FSC
www.fsc.org

Wayland, an imprint of
Hachette Children's Group
Part of Hodder and Stoughton
Carmelite House
50 Victoria Embankment
London EC4Y 0DZ

An Hachette UK Company

www.hachette.co.uk
www.hachettechildrens.co.uk

The website addresses (URLs) included in this book were valid at the time of going to press. However, it is possible that contents or addresses may have changed since the publication of this book. No responsibility for any such changes can be accepted by either the author or the Publisher.

Note: In preparation of this book, all due care has been exercised with regard to the instructions, activities and techniques depicted. The publishers regret that they can accept no liability for any loss or injury sustained. Always get adult supervision and follow manufacturers' advice when using electric and battery-powered appliances.

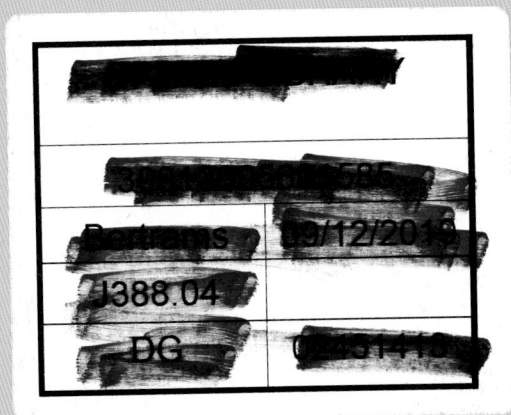

Bertrams 09/12/2019
J388.04
DG

CONTENTS

On the move! 4
Elastic band car 6
Paddle boat 8
Cable car 10
Propeller plane 12
Going up! 16
Helicopter 18
Jetpack 22
Maglev train 24
Multi-mode transport hub 26

And here is your finished transport hub! 28

Glossary and further information 30
Index 32

ON THE MOVE!

Humans have always needed to travel. We had to move around to find food and building materials, trade with our neighbours or to explore. For many thousands of years, though, we mainly got around by walking and most people didn't go far.

But eventually, we began to invent some faster and easier ways of moving, and transport took off! Transport past and present includes:

- Boats for floating to and fro on rivers and seas
- Training and taming animals, like elephants and horses, to carry us around
- Super-useful wheeled vehicles, which were first invented about 5,000 years ago, and now include cars, bikes, buses, trucks and trains
- Several ways of flying, from hot air balloons to planes, helicopters and jetpacks.

If you love trains, planes, cars and other types of transport, this book is for you. It shows you how to make transport models of many kinds – and many of them really work as well!

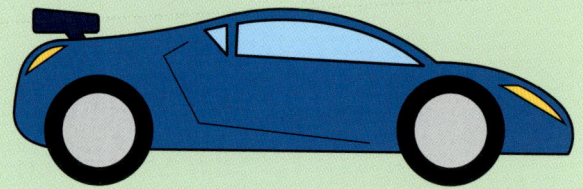

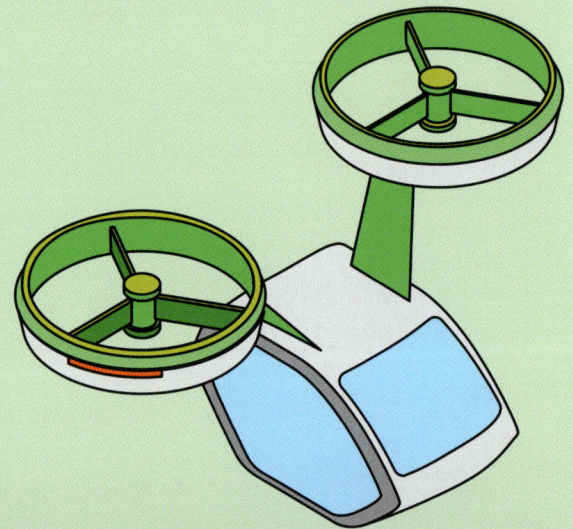

BE A TRANSPORT ENGINEER!

You can follow the instructions exactly and make the projects just as they are in the book – but you don't have to. You're also free to use the instructions as a starting point and design your own travel technology, just like the genius inventors of the past and the transport engineers of today.

For example, you could develop the car project (pages 6–7) to make other kinds of wheeled vehicles or design a hi-tech car, wheelchair or bus of the future. Try making a submarine instead of a boat (see pages 8–9), use maglev technology (see pages 24–25) to design and make a hoverboard, or see if it's possible to combine a plane and a helicopter (see pages 12–15 and 18–21). The sky's the limit!

MAKER MATERIALS

The projects in the book have been designed to work using things you can find at home, such as boxes, packaging and basic art and craft equipment. If you don't have what you need, you can usually get it at a hobby or craft store, supermarket or DIY store, or by ordering online. See page 31 for a list of useful sources.

Charity shops are a great place to look for old, cheap household items and craft materials.

BLOOP BLOOP! SAFETY ALERT!

For some of the projects, you'll need to use sharp tools such as a craft knife or an electric appliance like a hot glue gun.

For anything involving sharp objects, heat or electricity, always ask an adult to help and supervise. Make sure you keep items like these in a safe place, away from where younger children could find them.

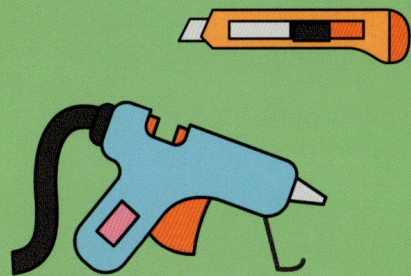

CAN I USE THIS?

Before you start emptying the cupboards, make sure any containers or other household items you want to use are finished with, clean and you have permission to use them to make a variety of vehicles to travel the world in. Let's get going!

ELASTIC BAND CAR

Around the world, over a billion cars carry people from A to B every day. This easy-to-make model is powered not by petrol, but with an elastic band, making it zoom around at high speed.

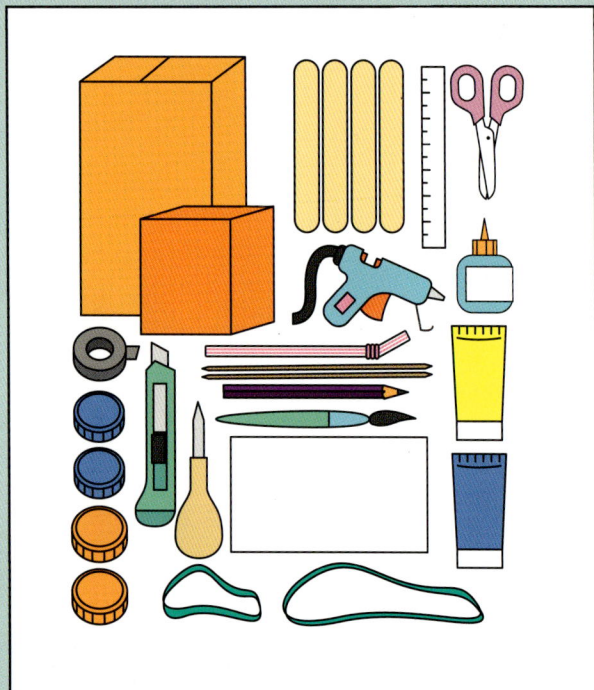

WHAT YOU NEED

- A small rectangular cardboard box
- Another smaller box
- A ruler
- Four lolly sticks or craft sticks
- Strong glue or a glue gun
- Strong sticky tape
- Scissors or a craft knife
- A plastic or paper straw
- Wooden skewers
- Two matching pairs of round plastic bottle or container lids
- A bradawl or thick needle
- Smooth card
- Long, thin elastic bands
- Short, wide elastic bands (optional)
- Paint and paintbrushes (optional)

If you have one larger and one smaller set of lids, use the bigger ones for the back wheels.

1 Measure the width of the main cardboard box. Cut two sticks to the same length as the width of the box, using a craft knife or strong scissors. Glue them to two other sticks at right angles, to make a frame but glue one of the short sticks 4 cm in from one end of the frame.

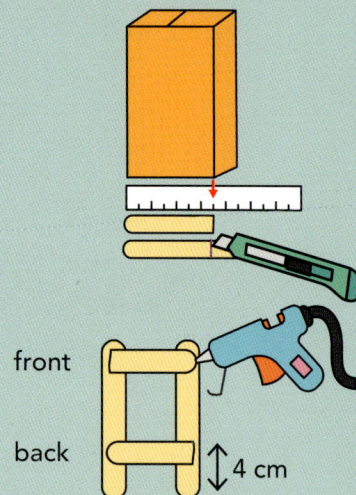

front

back

4 cm

2 Flip the frame over. Cut a piece of straw as wide as the frame. Glue it across the front of the frame. Cut two shorter pieces as wide as the craft sticks. Glue them across the two sticks at the back end.

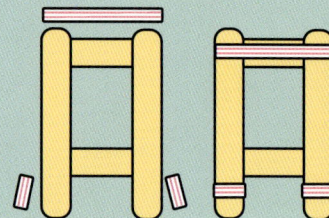

3 Use tape to fix the straws on more firmly. Cut two lengths of wooden skewer, the width of the frame, plus an extra 3 cm. Thread them through the straws to make two axles.

3 cm

4 Make a hole through the middle of each plastic lid, using the bradawl or thick needle. Push the wheels onto the ends of the wooden skewer axles, so that they almost touch the frame.

6 Find an elastic band that's longer than the frame or tie several together (see page 14). Loop one end of the elastic band around the front of the frame (not the axle) and push the other end of the elastic band through the loop. Pull it tight. Tie the other end around the rear axle and fix it in place with glue.

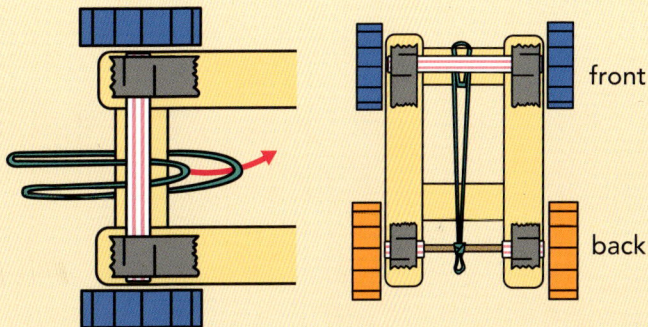

front

back

7 If you have short, wide elastic bands, stretch them around the back wheels to give extra grip. Turn the car frame over so the axles are underneath. Test the car by pulling it back on a flat surface to wind up the elastic band around the back axle. Now let it go!

8 Cut out the underneath of the larger box. This will keep it clear of the elastic band. Glue it on top of the frame. For the top part of the car, carefully cut windows and a windscreen out of the smaller box, and glue it on top. Paint the car too, if you like.

TIP

For a curved roof, use a section of cardboard tube. Cut along one side and open it out into a semicircle. Cut semicircles of card to make sides and glue them to the curved roof. Cut out windows.

TAKE IT FURTHER ...

You can use the same method to design and make other vehicles, such as a truck, a bus, a racing car or a camper van!

PADDLE BOAT

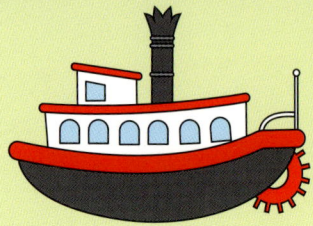

In the 1800s, big paddle steamers were a common sight. Today most ships have underwater propellers, but many lakes and rivers still have paddle boats for tourists. The paddle is at the back of the boat, and turns like a waterwheel to push the boat forward.

WHAT YOU NEED

- A plastic washing-up liquid bottle, shampoo bottle or similar, with a flattened shape and a lid
- A pack of lolly sticks or craft sticks
- Marker pens
- Scissors or a craft knife
- Strong glue or a glue gun
- A small plastic container, such as a dessert or snack pot
- A round, tube-shaped bottle lid
- An elastic band
- A piece of stiff, flat plastic, such as the lid from an ice cream or margarine tub
- Small plain stickers (optional)

1 Peel any labels or stickers off the bottle. With a marker pen, draw along the sides of the bottle, curving upward around the lid and at the back, to make a boat shape.

2 With an adult's help, cut out the boat shape as neatly as possible. This is your boat's hull. Check it floats well on water. (If not, try again with another bottle!)

3 Take the remaining part of the bottle and cut around it, to make a smaller boat shape about 1 cm deep. This should fit inside your boat to make a platform.

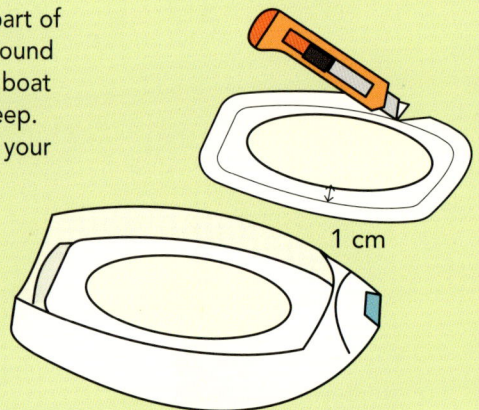

1 cm

4 On a flat surface, arrange lolly or craft sticks to make a deck, as wide as your boat's hull but slightly longer. Glue on more sticks at an angle to fix the sticks together. Leave to dry.

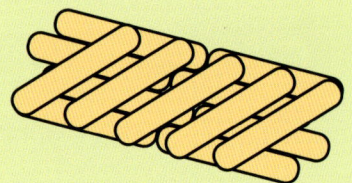

5 Put the platform you made in step 3 onto the deck and draw around it. With an adult's help, cut out the deck with strong scissors or a craft knife. Put the platform back in the boat and glue the deck on top.

6 Glue your plastic pot on top of the deck. Add windows using stickers or a marker pen. Glue the tube-shaped lid on top of the pot to make a funnel.

7 Take two more sticks and cut small notches in the ends. Glue the sticks to the sides of the boat, at the back, so that the notched ends stick out at least 5 cm.

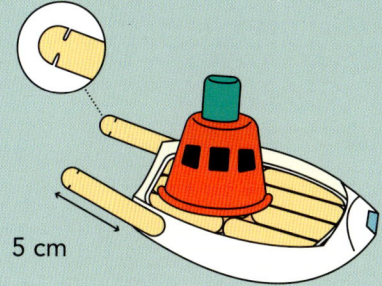

5 cm

8 Loop an elastic band between the sticks where the notches are. Cut a paddle from the stiff plastic, about 3 cm wide and 8 cm long.

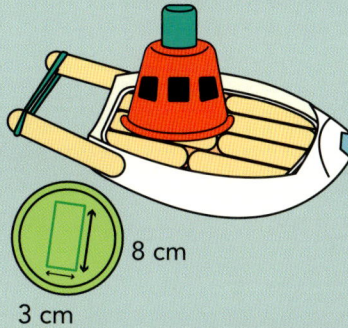

8 cm

3 cm

9 Fit the paddle between the two sides of the elastic band, and wind it up by twisting it round and round. Put the boat in shallow water, in a bath for example, and let it go!

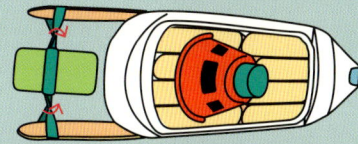

THE SCIENCE BIT!

To work, the paddle has to stick out of the water, so that it only pushes against the water in one direction. That's why paddle boats are not great on stormy seas, but perfect for lakes and slow, wide rivers.

TIP

If the boat goes backwards, you need to twist the paddle the other way!

CABLE CAR

Few modes of transport are as exciting (or for some people, as terrifying!) as a soaring, swinging cable car, carrying you high over valleys, rivers or icy ski slopes.

WHAT YOU NEED

- Two cardboard ribbon reels (or make your own – see yellow box)
- Four large metal paper clips
- A ball of string
- Scissors or a craft knife
- Several small cardboard or plastic boxes, similar in size and shape
- A marker pen
- Strong card
- Strong glue or sticky tape
- Fixed anchor points, such as banisters or coat hooks
- Stickers, coloured paper, markers, or paints and paintbrushes (optional)

Make sure you tie the cable car to fixed objects such as banisters or coat hooks, and ask an adult first. Don't use objects that can move or fall over, such as a chair or bookshelf.

CARDBOARD REELS

Ribbon reels hold ribbon, elastic or trim, and are sold at sewing and hobby stores. If you don't have any, you can make them from circles of thick cardboard.

1 Cut two larger circles and three slightly smaller ones.

2 Cut large holes in the middle of all the circles.

3 Glue them together with the smaller circles sandwiched between the big ones.

4 Wrap tape around the inside to make it smooth.

1 Straighten out the paper clips and shape them into hooks. Make a small hook on one end and on the other end, a hook big enough to fit onto your reels. Fit two hooks into each reel.

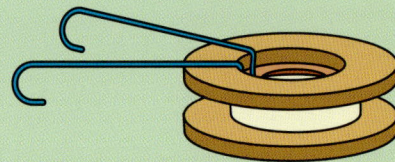

2 Cut four pieces of string about 30 cm long. Use them to tie the hooks to banisters or other fixed objects, with the two reels some distance apart.

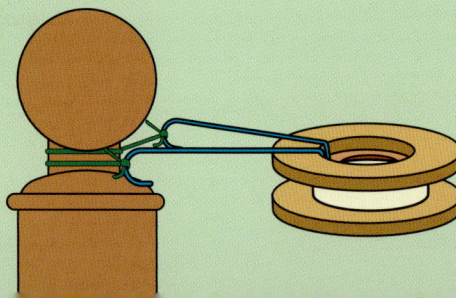

3 Cut a very long piece of string, more than twice the distance between the two reels. Thread it around the reels and tie the ends together to make a fairly tight loop of string linking the reels together.

4 Test the cable by pulling the string towards one of the reels. It should be able to move around in a loop.

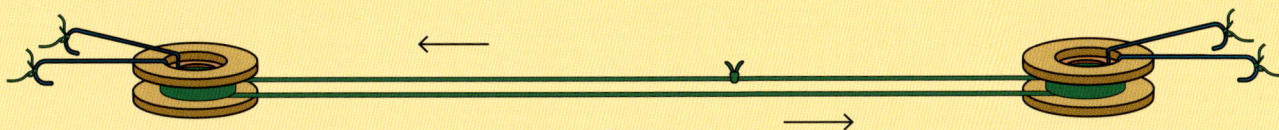

5 For a cable car, take a small box and draw windows onto the top half of it. Carefully cut them out. You can also paint the cable car or decorate it with paper, stickers or markers.

6 Cut a 1-cm-wide and 5-cm-long strip of strong card. Fold it in half and fold up the ends into tabs. Glue the tabs to the top of your cable car and make sure the top is secured so it won't open.

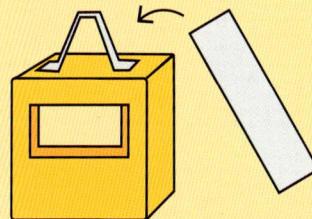

7 Cut a 20-cm length of string and tie one end around the cable car hanger. Tie the other end to the long cable loop, making sure the car has space to dangle freely.

8 Repeat step 5 and 6 to make more cable cars. Tie them to the loop, spaced out evenly around it. Pull gently on the cable to make them travel around the loop.

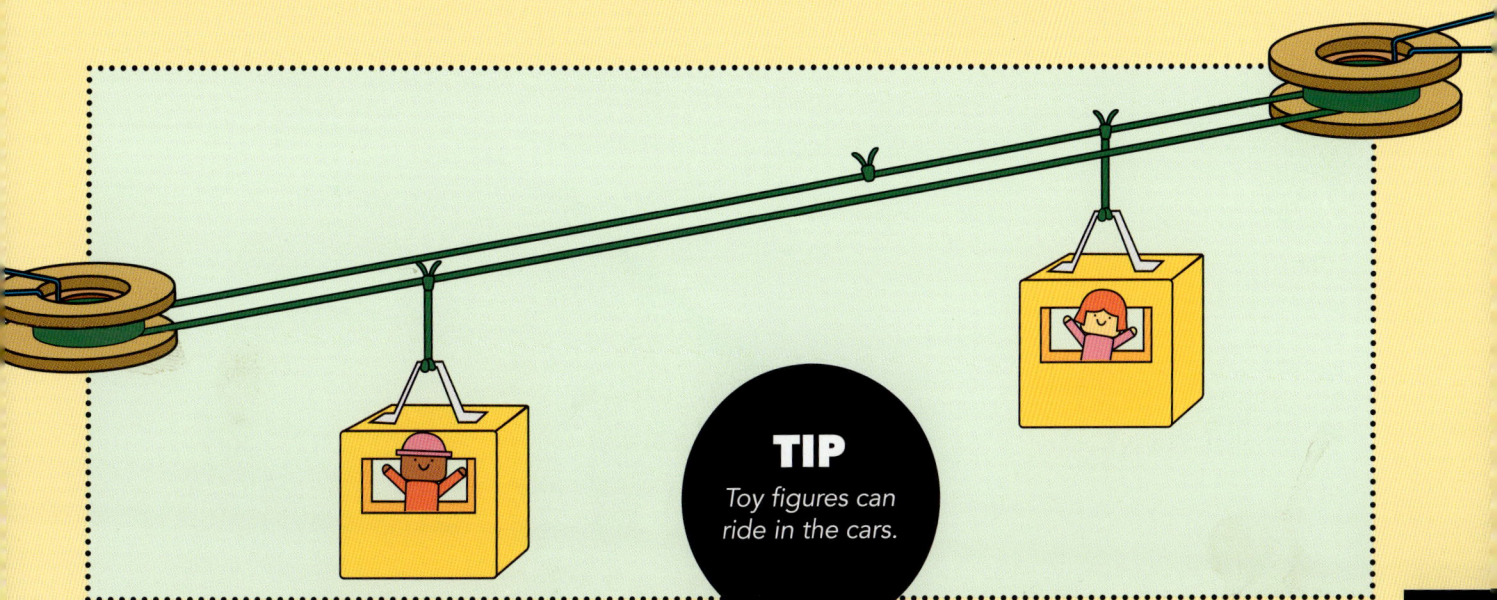

TIP
Toy figures can ride in the cars.

PROPELLER PLANE

The plane that made the first ever continuous, powered flight was driven by a propeller. It was the *Wright Flyer*, built by brothers Orville and Wilbur Wright, and it was flown in 1903. Since then, flying has really taken off!

WHAT YOU NEED

- Four or more long wooden skewers
- A paper or plastic straw
- Scissors or a craft knife
- Strong glue or a glue gun
- A piece of stiff, flat plastic, such as the lid from an ice cream or margarine tub
- A marker pen
- A bradawl or thick needle
- An eraser
- A paper or plastic disposable cup
- Strong sticky tape or duct tape
- An old, cheap ballpoint pen with a plastic ink tube inside
- A metal paper clip
- A long, thin elastic band (or several shorter ones)
- A4 plain paper sheets (any colour)
- PVA glue

1 Line up two wooden skewers side by side, with the pointed ends together. Cut two 1-cm sections of straw.

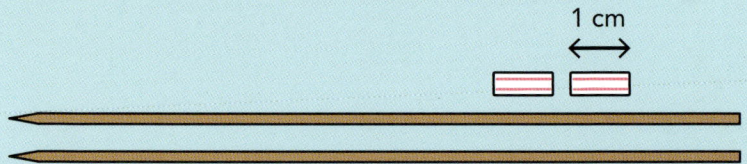

1 cm

2 Glue the pieces of straw in between the two skewers, at the ends. If your glue isn't super-strong, use small strips of tape to hold the skewers and straws together too.

3 Draw a small circle on the stiff plastic, about 1 cm across. Cut it out. Use the bradawl or thick needle to make a hole in the middle of it. When pushing the sharp tip through, put the eraser on the other side for it to stick into.

TIP

It's easiest to make this project work well if you have a glue gun. You can buy them cheaply at hobby stores, along with refills of glue sticks. Glue guns need to be plugged in and get hot, so ask an adult to help.

4 Carefully glue the circle of plastic onto the flat end of the skewers. Make sure the hole in the middle lines up with the end of the straw. Don't get glue on the hole or the straw.

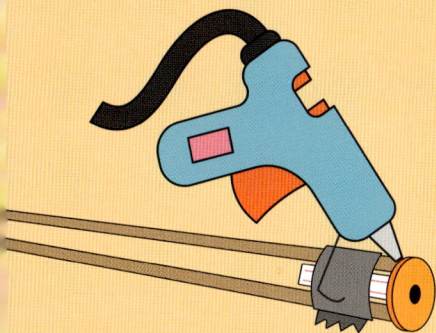

5 Draw two propeller blades on the side of the disposable cup. Use the full length of the cup to make them as long as possible. Carefully cut them out.

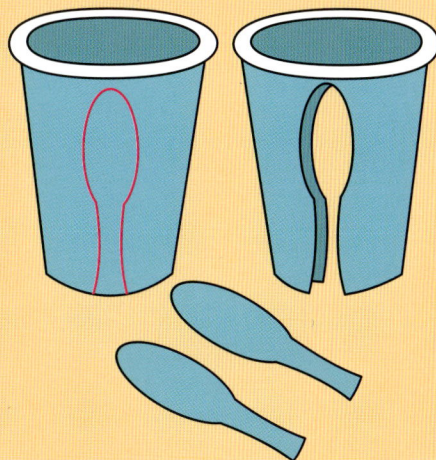

6 Cut a 5-cm-long piece from another wooden skewer. Take the ink tube out of the ballpoint pen. Cut a 1-cm-long piece off the end.

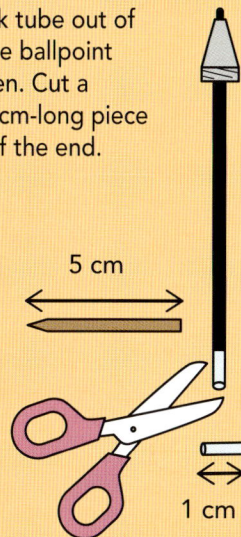

5 cm

1 cm

7 Glue the two propeller blades onto the ends of the piece of skewer, at a slight angle to each other. Leave a 1 cm gap in the middle. Strengthen the joins with tape.

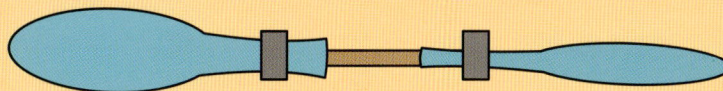

The blades have to be angled like this to push air backwards as they spin around.

8 Now glue the piece of ink tube onto the middle of the propeller. It should be in between the propeller blades.

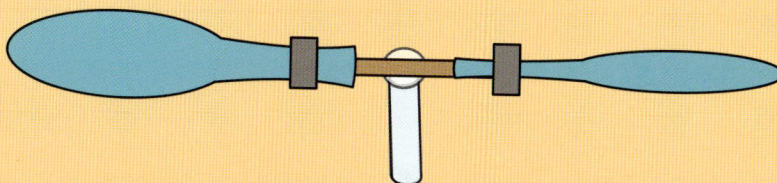

9 Straighten your metal paper clip. Bend one end over to make a narrow hook. Push the straight end through the straw at the flat end of the skewers and the hole in the plastic circle, so the hook is between the skewers.

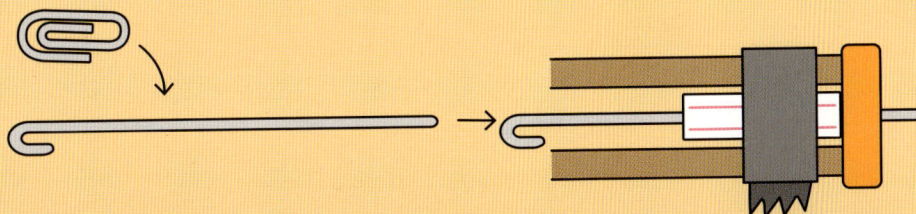

TURN THE PAGE TO CONTINUE ...

10 Dab a little glue onto the straight end of the paperclip. Push it into the ink tube attached to the propeller. Leave it to dry. Make sure no glue touches the plastic circle.

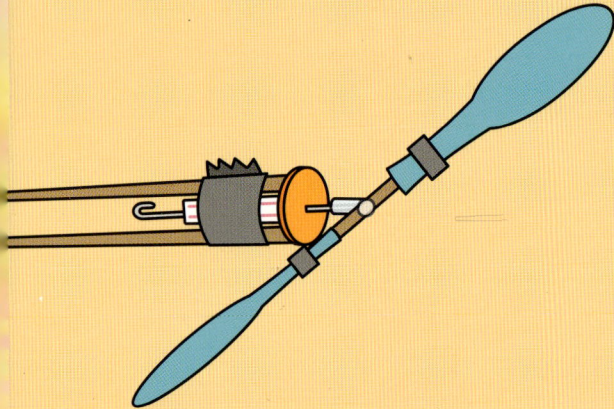

11 Find a long, thin elastic band at least as long as the skewers. Or, if you don't have one, loop two or more short, thin elastic bands together.

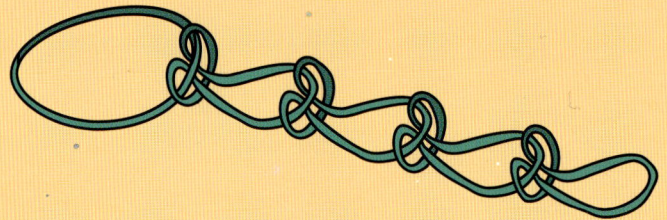

12 Hook one end of your elastic band on to the paper clip hook. Push the other end through the straw at the pointed end of the skewers (the back end of the plane).

13 Cut a short piece from another skewer, about 1 cm long. Push this through the elastic band so it sits horizontally against the straw at the back of the plane.

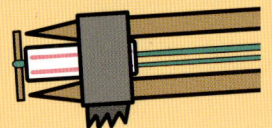

14 Add a dab of glue to hold the elastic band and the piece of skewer in place. When it's dry, test the propeller by twisting it round and round with your finger, then letting go.

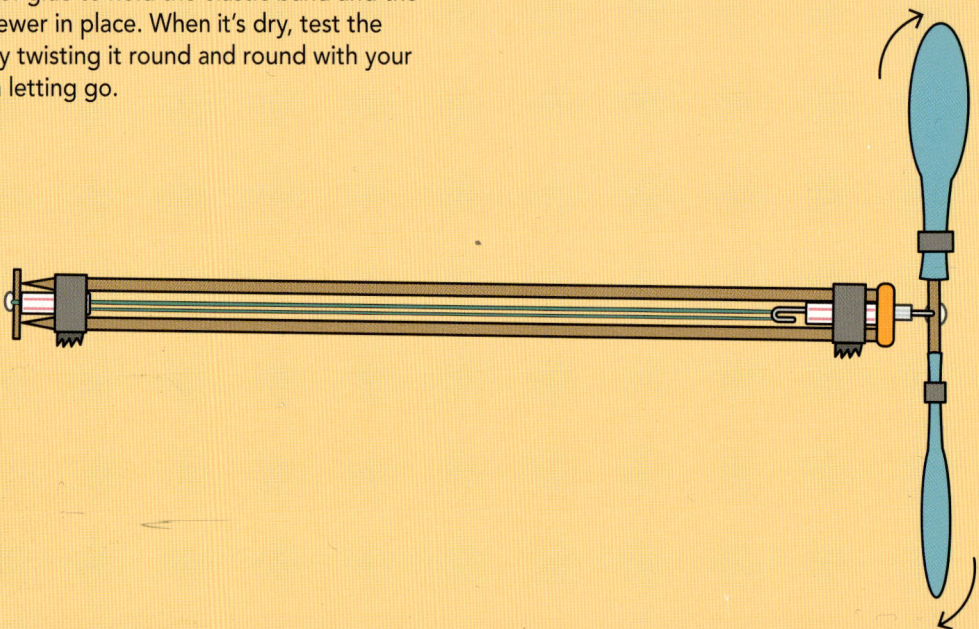

15 Make the wings by folding a piece of A4 paper in half lengthwise. Unfold the paper. Glue a wooden skewer along the fold, using strong glue. Fold the paper in half over the stick and glue it together with PVA glue.

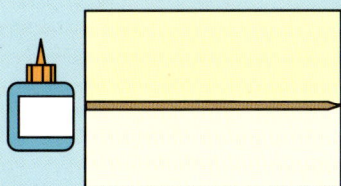

16 Where both edges of the piece of paper meet, fold a 1-cm strip upwards. Decorate the wings with logos or symbols if you like.

17 To make the tailplane, cut a piece of A4 paper in half lengthwise. Fold it in half along its length. Glue together with paper glue. Fold about 3 cm at each end of the tailplane upwards.

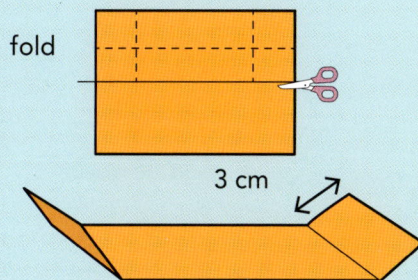

1 cm

fold

3 cm

18 Position the plane body with the skewers above one another (not flat). Use strong glue to glue the wings and the tailplane onto the upper skewer. The wings should be just in front of the middle and the tailplane right on the back end.

THE SCIENCE BIT!

As the propeller spins, the leading edge (furthest forward edge) of each propeller blade should come first. This allows the propeller to cut into the air and push the air backwards. If you wind up the propeller the wrong way round, it won't pull the plane forward. Try experimenting with both directions.

TIP

Fly the plane by winding up the propeller until the elastic is tightly wound. Hold it up high and launch into the air, angling the wings very slightly upwards.

GOING UP!

Of course, transport isn't just about zooming to and fro. Sometimes you also need to go up and down – to the top of a skyscraper, or the bottom of a mine. That's where lifts, also called elevators, come in very handy.

WHAT YOU NEED

- A long cardboard box or tube, such as a crisp tube
- A smaller box or tube that fits inside the first one
- Sticky tape
- Scissors or a craft knife
- Strong card
- Strong glue or a glue gun
- A bradawl or thick needle
- A marker pen
- String
- A wooden chopstick, pencil or wooden skewer
- Stickers, coloured paper or paints and paintbrushes (optional)

1 Use the small box or tube to make the lift itself. Draw a doorway on the front of it, and carefully cut it out.

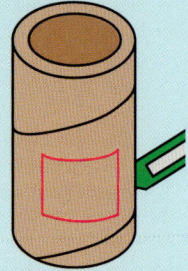

2 Tape down the lid or flaps of the box. If you're using a piece of tube or a box that needs a base, draw around it onto card. Cut out the shape and glue it in place.

3 Use the bradawl or thick needle to make two holes through the top edges of the lift, one on each side. Cut two pieces of string at least twice as long as the height of your larger box or tube. Thread and tie the ends of the strings to the holes in the lift.

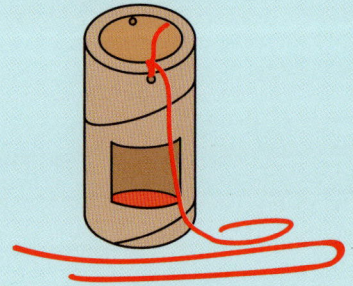

4 On a piece of card, draw a rectangle slightly larger than your lift door. Cut it out, and draw around it onto the larger box or tube to mark two openings, one at the bottom and one higher up (but not right at the top).

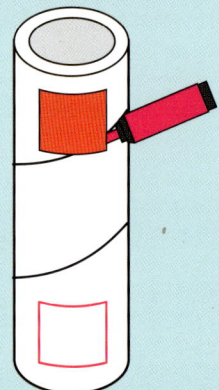

5 Carefully cut out the openings. Lower the lift into the larger tube or box to check it can move up and down and lines up with the openings. Leave the ends of the strings hanging out. Decorate the tube or box if you like.

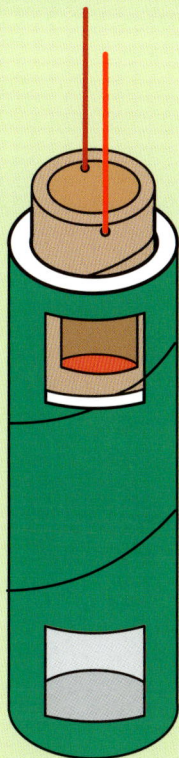

6 Cut four rectangular cardboard shapes about 3 cm wide and 5 cm long with a curve at one end. Use a bradawl or needle to make holes in the curved ends, large enough for a chopstick or skewer. Glue them onto the sides of the larger box or tube at the top, in pairs, one on the inside and one on the outside.

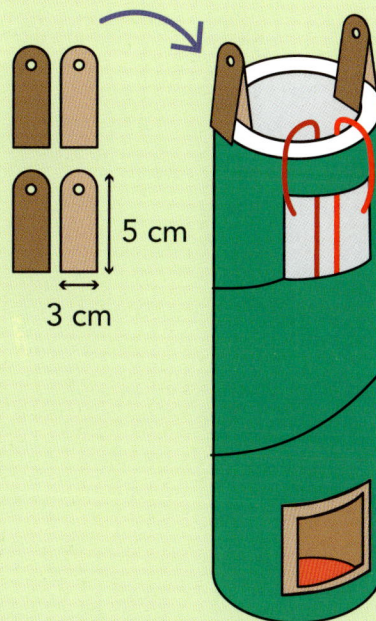

5 cm

3 cm

7 Push the chopstick or skewer through both holes, so that it is held in place above the top of the tube. Lift up the ends of the two strings and check they're the same length. If not, trim them so that they are.

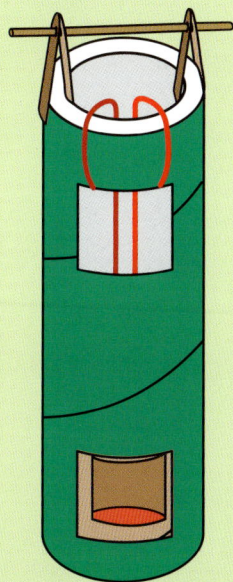

8 Tie the ends of the strings around the skewer, with a little glue to hold them in place. When it's dry, turn the skewer to wind up the strings until they are tight. You can then turn the skewer to raise or lower the lift.

TAKE IT FURTHER ...
Can you add a door to the lift that opens and closes?

HELICOPTER

Helicopters don't fly fast, but they are incredibly useful. Because they can take off and land without a runway, and hover in mid-air, they are perfect for search and rescue missions and for transport to and from hard-to-reach places, like oil rigs or tiny islands.

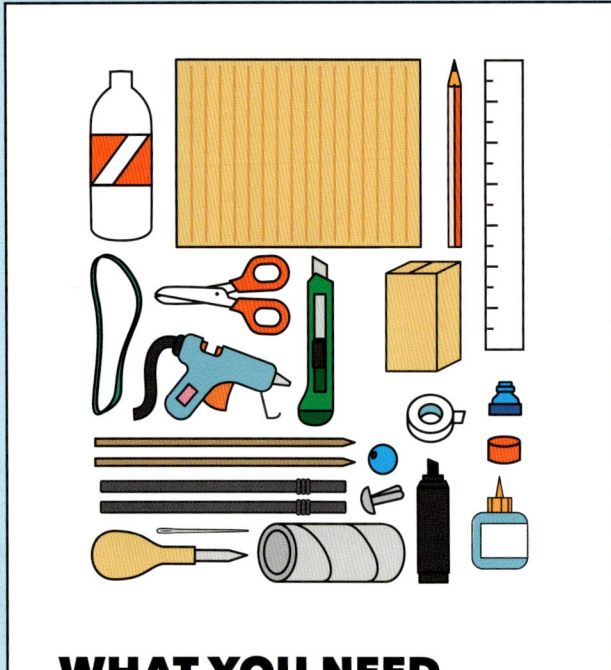

WHAT YOU NEED

- A clear disposable plastic fizzy drink bottle
- A ruler and a pencil
- Card or corrugated cardboard
- A black marker pen
- Scissors or a craft knife
- Strong glue or a glue gun
- Strong sticky tape
- A split pin fastener
- A small cardboard box, narrower than the bottle.
- Long wooden skewers
- A small round bead or button
- A cardboard tube, such as a kitchen roll tube
- A bradawl or thick needle
- A long elastic band (or several smaller ones)
- A round bottle lid and the lid from a disposable bottle with a 'sports' spout
- Two bendy straws

1 Measure the width of your bottle. On a large piece of card, draw a shape like the one below, with a central bottle shape as wide as your bottle and two large flaps at the sides.

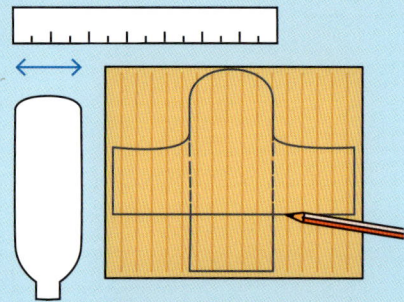

2 Cut out the shape. Use the ruler and pencil to score the fold lines. Fold the sides up. Sit your bottle in the middle, with the front of the bottle sticking out at the curved end of the shape.

3 Curve the side flaps over the bottle. Trim off any extra card, leaving just a small overlap. Tape the card together over the top of the bottle.

4 Hold your bottle so that the right amount is sticking out at the front to make a curved helicopter cabin. Mark a line at the point where where it meets the card. Take the bottle out and cut off the top end 1 cm below the line.

5 Ask an adult to help you carefully cut the neck off the bottle, to leave a rounded shape. Glue the edge of the bottle in place inside the cardboard, to make your helicopter body. You should be able to reach inside it from the back.

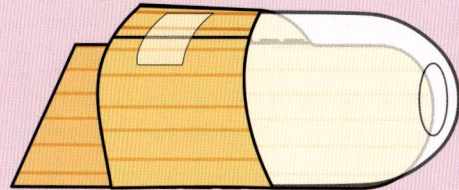

1 cm

6 Cut the corner off a small cardboard box. This is your seat.

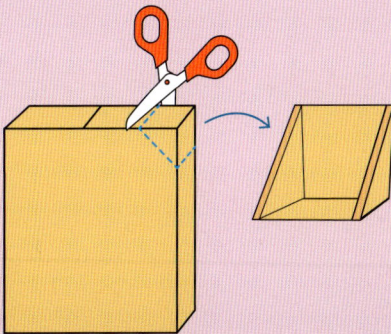

7 Cut a square of cardboard the same width as the seat. Fold it into a rectangular box shape and glue it together. This is the control panel, you can decorate it with stickers or pens.

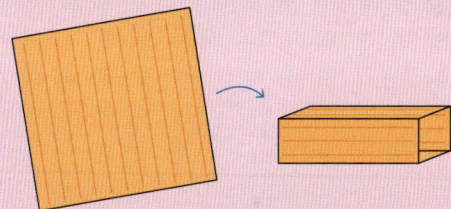

8 Put the control panel in the seat and glue it in place. Cut a 3-cm piece of wooden skewer. Glue a bead or button onto one end. Stick the other end into the block to make a joystick.

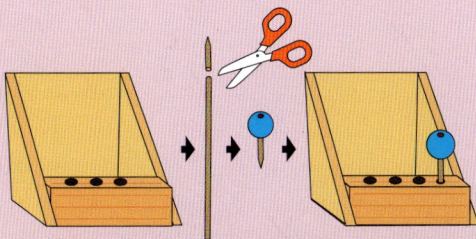

9 Put glue underneath the seat and place it inside the helicopter from the back.

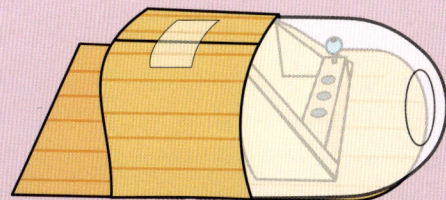

TURN THE PAGE TO CONTINUE ...

10 Cut the cardboard tube to the same height as the inside of the helicopter. Push it inside so that it fits between the roof and the floor, in the cardboard section.

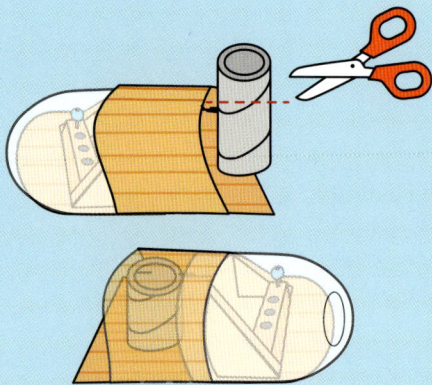

11 Use the bradawl or thick needle to make holes in the top and bottom of the helicopter, in the middle of where the cardboard tube is. Make the holes bigger with the point of a pair of scissors.

12 Find an elastic band that's as long as the helicopter's height or string shorter ones together (see page 14). Using a wooden skewer, push one end of the elastic band through the hole in the top of the helicopter and down through the bottom.

13 Cut a 2-cm piece of wooden skewer and loop it through the bottom end of the elastic band. Tape it to the bottom of the helicopter to hold it in place.

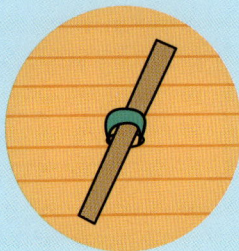

14 Make a hole through the middle of the regular bottle lid with the bradawl or thick needle. Make it bigger with scissors. Thread the elastic band up through it. Cut off the spout part of the sports bottle lid. Place it on top of the first lid.

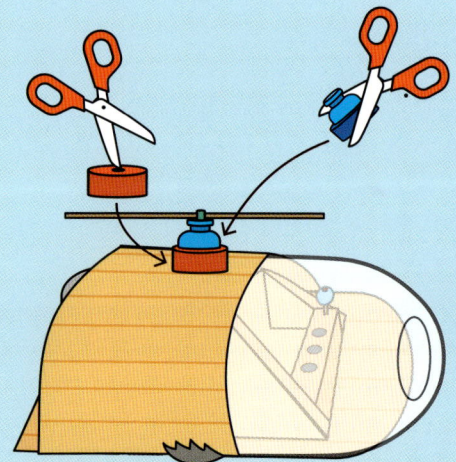

15 Thread the elastic band through the spout. You can use a skewer to help push the elastic through as in step 12. Glue the two lids down. Thread a long wooden skewer through the elastic band at the top.

16 Draw two long rotor blades on strong card, about 30 cm long. Cut them out.

17 Colour the rotor blades black with a black marker pen. Carefully glue them to the ends of the skewer, leaving a gap in the middle around the elastic band.

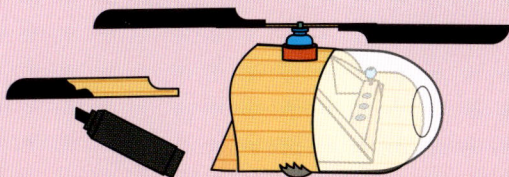

18 Draw and cut out a long triangle of card slightly longer than the body of your helicopter and about twice as wide as the helicopter is tall.

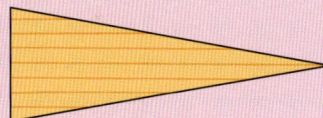

19 Curve the triangle over in the middle and glue the narrower end together to make a tail. Put the tail inside the back of the helicopter and glue to the inside of the cabin.

20 Cut out a small tail rotor shape from cardboard. Make holes through the middle of the rotor and the end of the tail. Fix them together with a split pin fastener, so that the rotor can spin around.

21 Draw two V-shaped sections of card for the helicopter's legs. Cut them out and glue them to the sides of the helicopter.

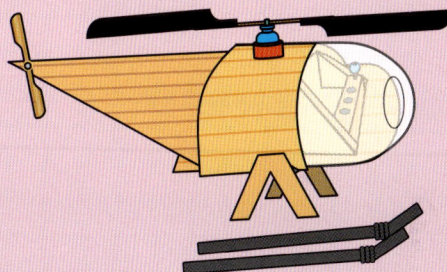

22 Bend the two bendy straws up at an angle. Glue the straws to the ends of the legs on each side of the helicopter, to make the landing skids.

TIP
You can leave the helicopter as it is, paint it or decorate it with markers or stickers.

TIP
To make the rotor blades turn, turn them around until the elastic band is tightly wound, and let go.

JETPACK

Imagine being able to take off into the air and fly wherever you like. One device that can help us do this is called a jetpack. So why don't we all have one? Well, they're hard to control, they don't go far and they're VERY expensive. You'll just have to make a model one instead!

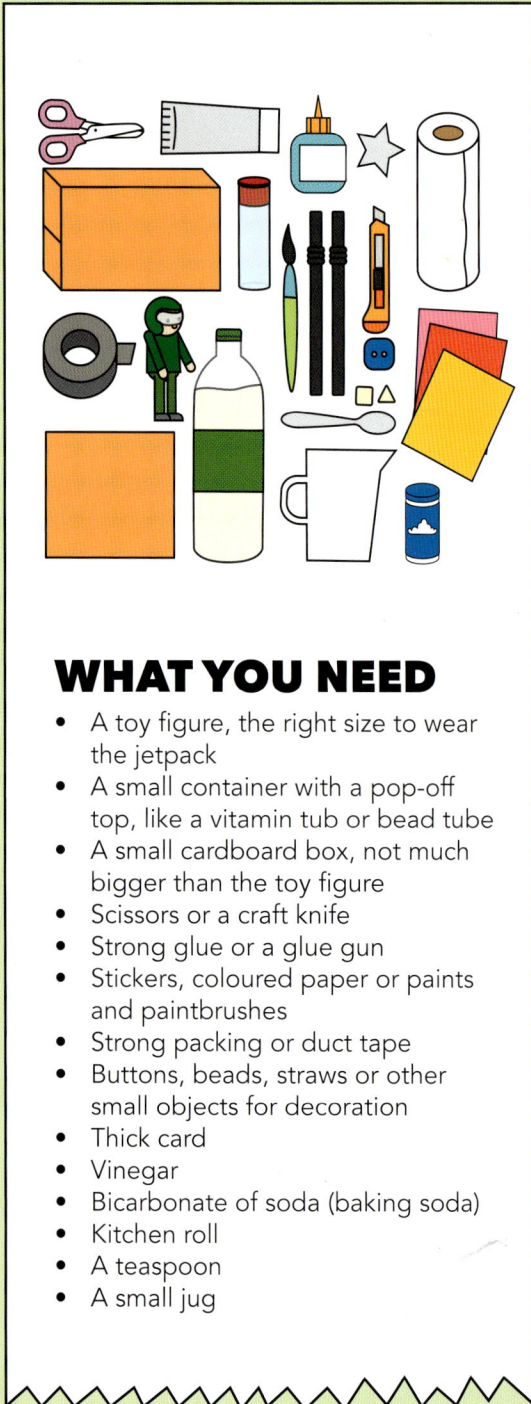

WHAT YOU NEED

- A toy figure, the right size to wear the jetpack
- A small container with a pop-off top, like a vitamin tub or bead tube
- A small cardboard box, not much bigger than the toy figure
- Scissors or a craft knife
- Strong glue or a glue gun
- Stickers, coloured paper or paints and paintbrushes
- Strong packing or duct tape
- Buttons, beads, straws or other small objects for decoration
- Thick card
- Vinegar
- Bicarbonate of soda (baking soda)
- Kitchen roll
- A teaspoon
- A small jug

1 Trim your cardboard box to the same length as your container. The bottom of the box should be open. Glue or tape any flaps at the top closed.

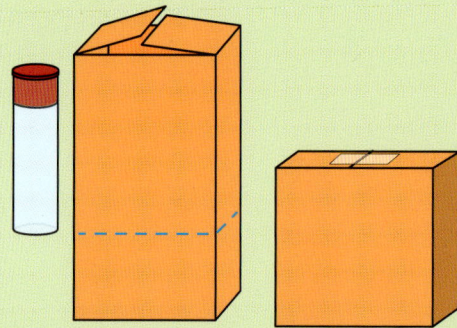

2 If you like, paint the box or cover it in paper. It can be any colour, but black, grey, white or silver are typical jetpack colours. Leave it to dry.

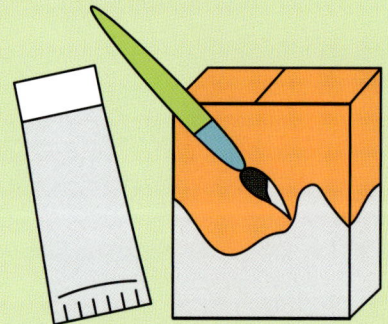

3 Glue on small buttons, beads, pieces of straw or other objects to look like controls. Some bent sections of bendy straws look good. You can also add stickers, lettering or a logo.

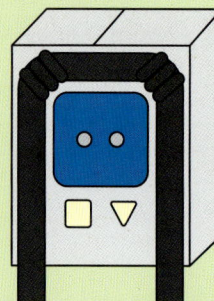

4 Remove the container lid and set it aside. Put the container inside the jetpack with the opening facing down. Cut pieces of thick card to fit inside the jetpack. Use them to fill any space around the container to hold it firmly in place.

5 Fold pieces of duct or packing tape lengthwise to make strong straps. Hold the jetpack against your toy figure's back, and fit one strap around its waist and one around its shoulders. Attach the ends to the jetpack with strong glue or tape.

6 Cut a piece of kitchen roll about 5 cm square. Put half a teaspoon of bicarbonate of soda in the middle and fold it up into a parcel.

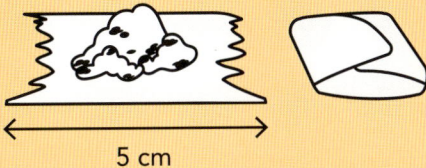

5 cm

7 Put a little vinegar into the jug. Hold the toy figure and jetpack upside down, and pour vinegar into the container until it's about half-full.

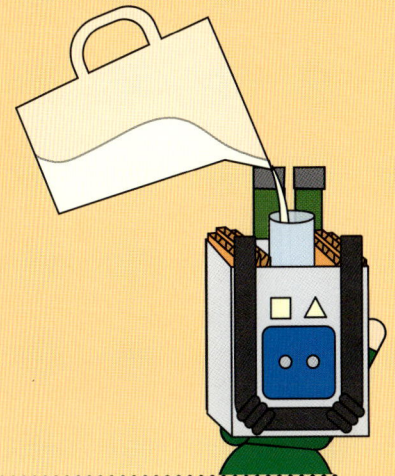

8 Push the kitchen roll parcel into the the container lid, put the lid into the upside-down tube, then quickly turn the toy figure and the jetpack over. Stand the toy on the ground. Step back and wait for take-off!

THE SCIENCE BIT!

This jetpack works using a chemical reaction. As the vinegar and bicarbonate of soda combine, they react and create carbon dioxide gas. It expands and forces the container open, making it shoot upwards.

TIP

Launch the jetpack outdoors, or somewhere easy to clean like a bathroom, as it's a bit messy.

MAGLEV TRAIN

If you hold two magnets next to each other, they will either attract each other or "repel" each other and push apart. Some types of train use this magnetic pushing force to hover above the track. They are "maglev" trains, short for magnetic levitation.

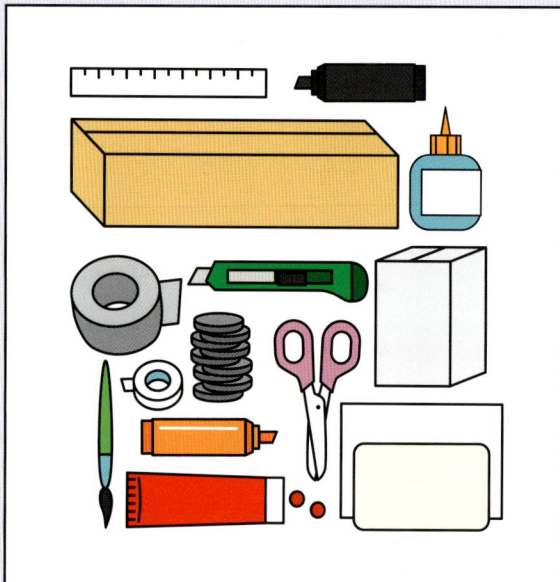

WHAT YOU NEED

- A large, strong corrugated cardboard box
- 30-40 ceramic disk magnets, 2 cm wide
- A ruler
- A marker pen
- Strong scissors or a craft knife
- Strong packing tape or duct tape
- Normal strength sticky tape
- A small cardboard box or smooth card
- Strong glue
- Stickers, paper, marker pens or paints and paintbrushes

For this project, you need magnets! It's usually easiest and cheapest to buy them online, but you might also find them in hobby, stationery or toy stores.

1 To make the track, measure and cut along the long edges of the box to make two 5-cm-wide L-shaped strips of cardboard that are as long as possible.

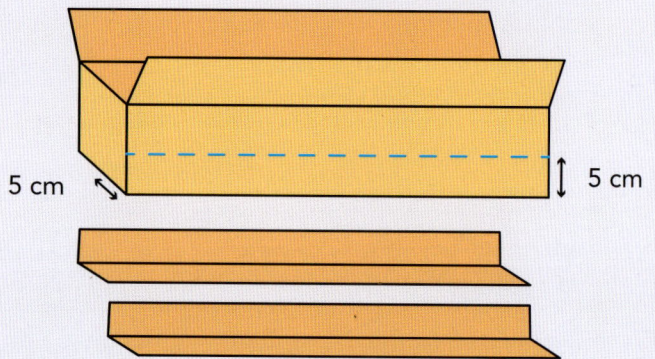

5 cm   5 cm

2 Mark and cut out a flat 5-cm-wide strip of card, the same length as the L-shaped strips. Unroll a long strip of packing or duct tape and lie it sticky-side up on the floor. Take one magnet and mark one side of it with a sticker or a piece of tape.

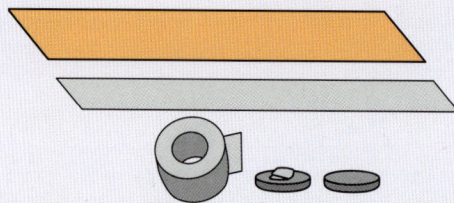

3 Before sticking the other magnets to the strip of tape in two rows, find the side that repels the marked side of the first magnet. Stick the tested magnet down with the repelling side facing upwards. This makes sure all the magnets on the strip are facing the same way.

4 Stop when you've used up all except four of your magnets. Unroll another strip of tape. Press it down on top of the magnets on the first strip, making a sandwich. Trim off the ends and lie the magnet sandwich down on the strip of card.

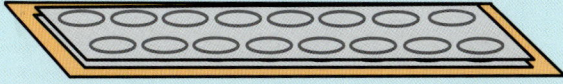

5 Use normal sticky tape to tape the magnet sandwich to the card, wrapping the tape around it to hold the magnets flat. Take the two L-shaped strips and push them together to make a channel. Lie the strip of magnets in the middle.

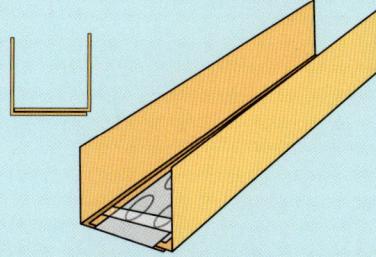

6 Mark and cut out two squares of strong card, 5 cm square, and fit them on to the ends of the track. Tape them on with strong tape. Cut another piece of card 5 cm wide and 10 cm long.

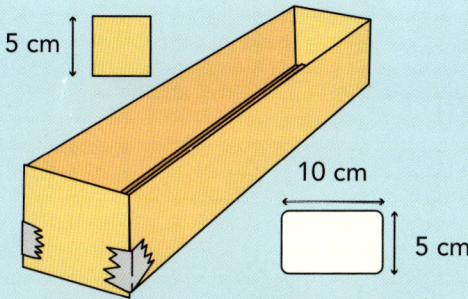

5 cm

10 cm

5 cm

7 Tape the last four magnets to the corners of the card. Make sure they all have the side that repels the other magnets facing down. You should now be able to put the card on the track so that it levitates above the strip of magnets.

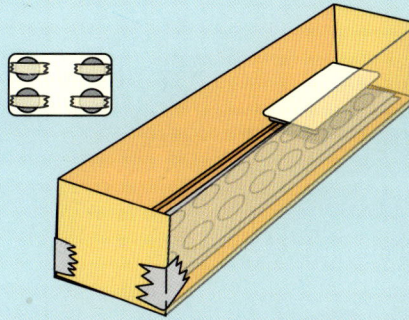

8 To make the train, use a small box just under 5 cm wide or make one by cutting and folding a piece of card. Decorate the train with paints, pens, paper or stickers, and glue it on top of the levitating card.

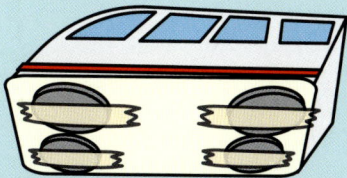

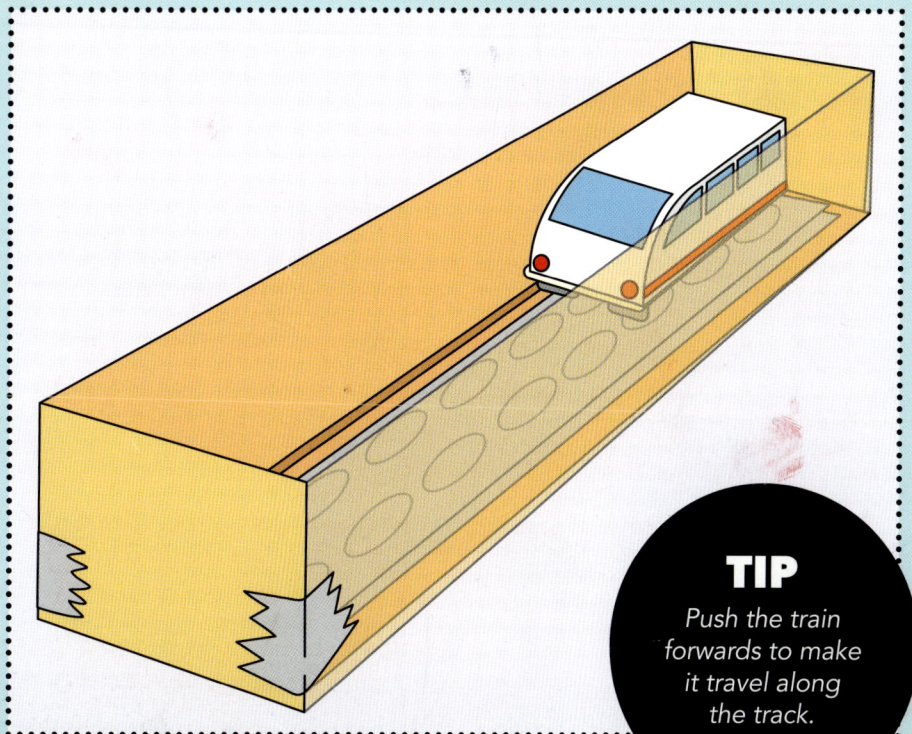

TIP

Push the train forwards to make it travel along the track.

MULTI-MODE TRANSPORT HUB

At a transport interchange, or hub, you can change from one type, or mode, of transport to another. For example, you could switch from bike or car to train, bus or tram. This super-hub has even more options!

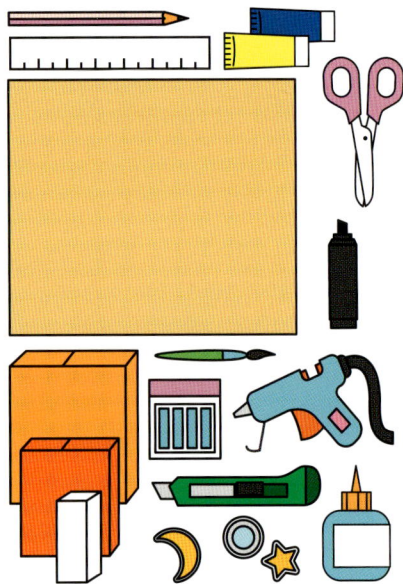

WHAT YOU NEED

- A very large piece of corrugated cardboard
- A marker pen
- Several cardboard boxes, such as cereal or cookie boxes
- Scissors or a craft knife
- A ruler and a pencil
- Strong glue or a glue gun
- Stickers, paper or paints and paintbrushes (optional)

You can get a big piece of cardboard from a box from a large appliance, such as a fridge. Or you can just tape several smaller pieces of cardboard together.

1 Along one side of the card, draw a road for your model car or other vehicles, with a pavement and a dotted line down the middle.

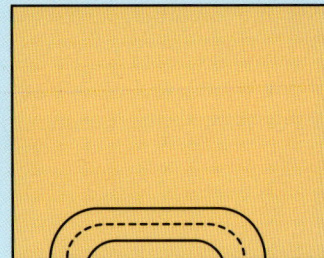

2 On the opposite side of the card, draw an airport runway for your plane, and a round helipad marked with an H shape for your helicopter.

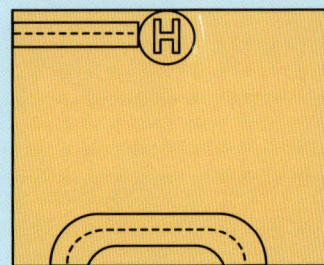

3 On another side, draw a river bank and a river, with a dock or jetty for your boat.

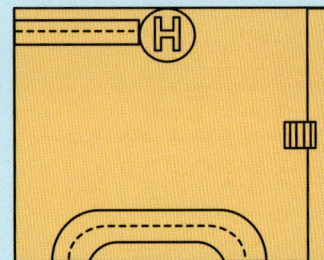

4 Now use boxes to make a ring of buildings in the middle, leading to the different areas. You can cut the tops off the boxes so you can see inside or leave them on if you prefer.

5 Next to the road, use a box to make an entrance hall, with doors cut into the front, and a big INTERCHANGE sign.

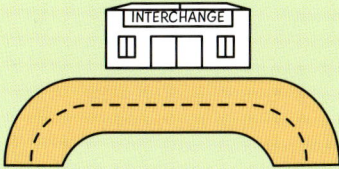

6 Use more boxes to make a train station, a train platform and a harbour station and a ticket office for the riverboat. Put signs on the doors leading out of the interchange, so passengers know where they're going.

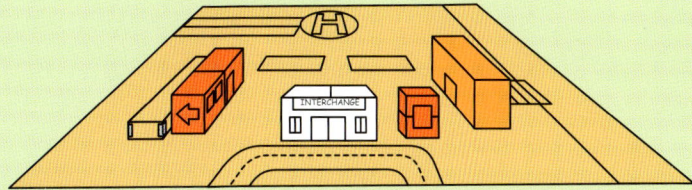

7 For the airport, make a two-storey building with one box on top of another. Cut a space in the middle for your lift. On the upper floor, cut out large windows to make a plane viewing area.

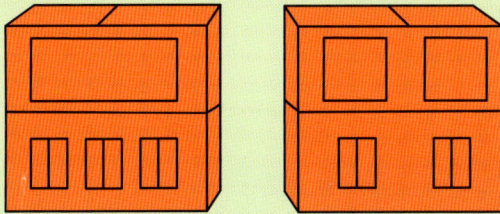

8 If you can position your interchange near your cable car, you could also use the upper floor as a cable car entry point. Cut a doorway and make a cable car sign.

9 Paint or decorate your interchange if you like, using paints, markers, stickers or paper.

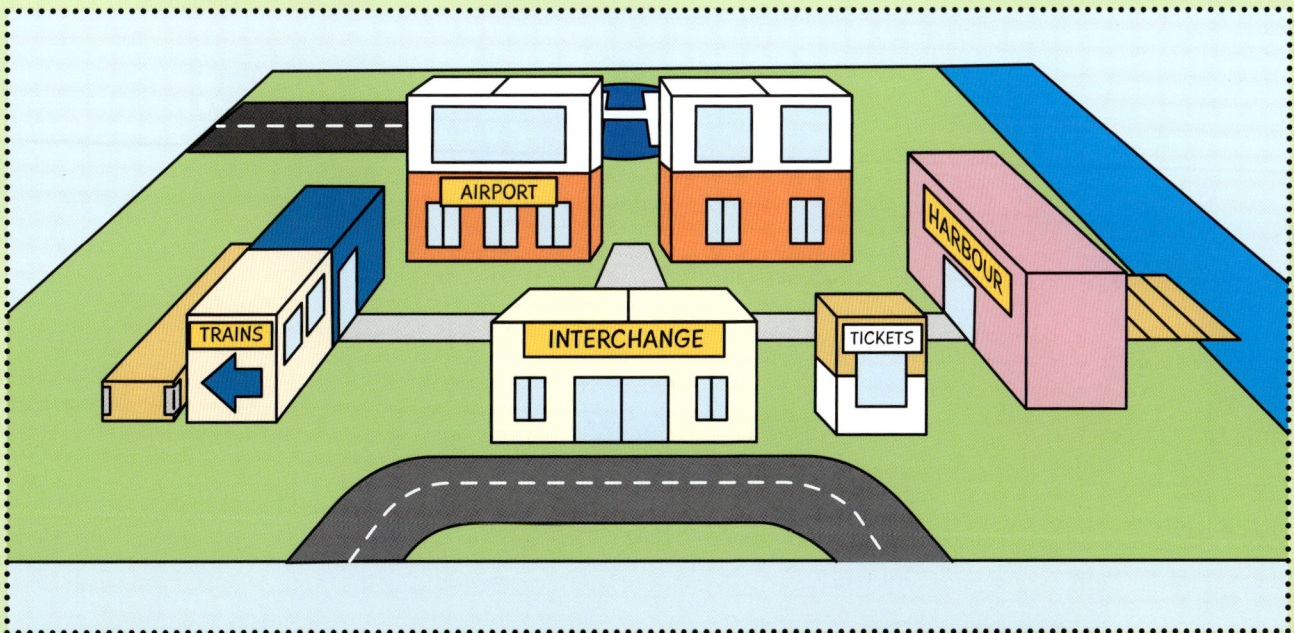

TAKE IT FURTHER ...

What else could you add? How about a waiting area with some benches, a lost property office, a bus stop on the road, a little cafe area with tables and a big information board showing arrivals and departures.

AND HERE IS YOUR FINISHED TRANSPORT HUB!

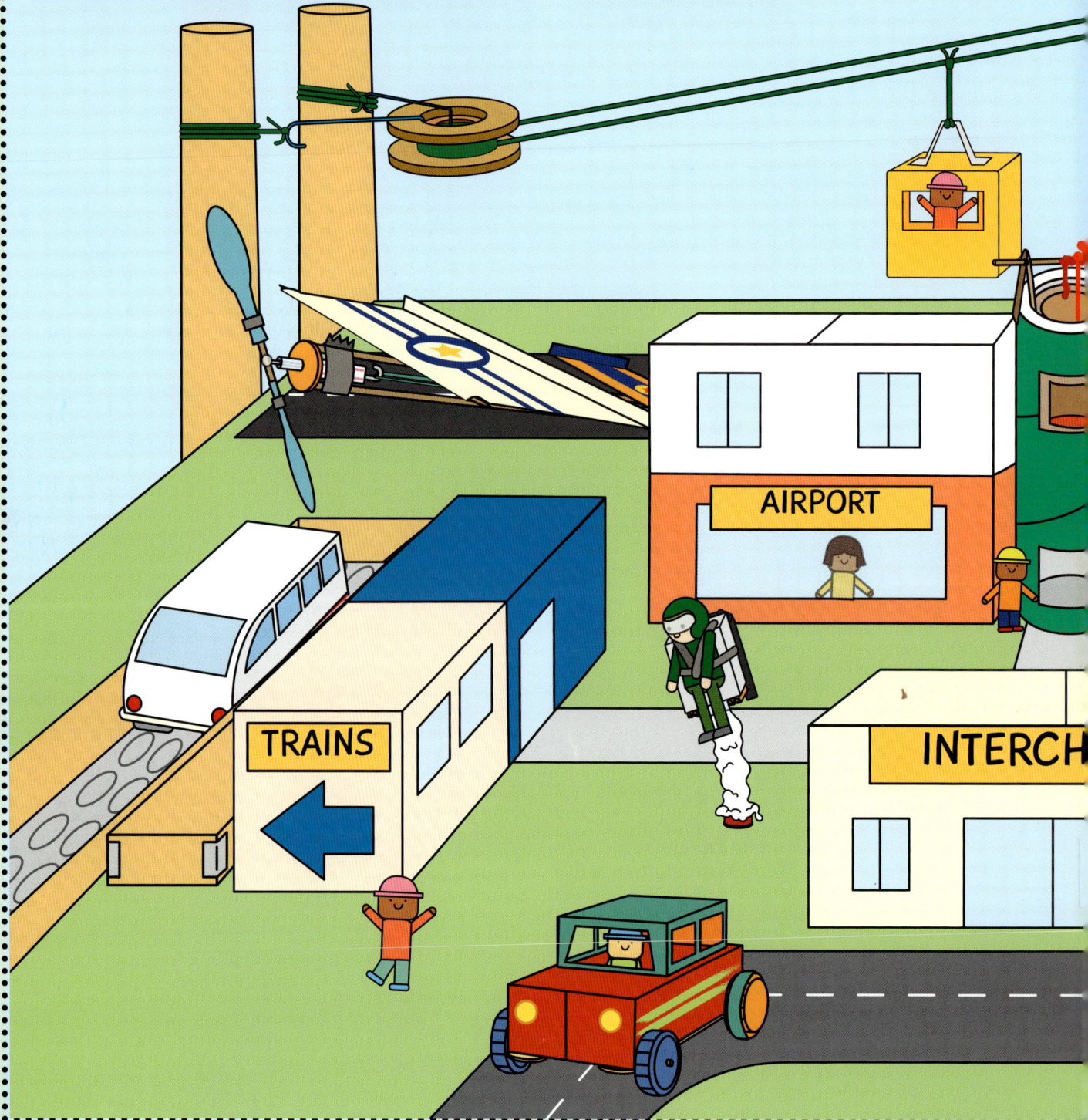

AIRPORT

TRAINS

INTERCH

HARBOUR

TICKETS

GE

GLOSSARY

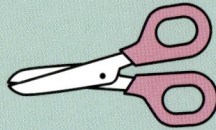

Attract To pull on something, as magnets do when they pull towards each other.

Axle A bar connected to the centre of a wheel that allows or causes it to turn, especially one connecting two wheels of a vehicle.

Bradawl A sharp, pointed tool for making neat holes.

Cabin The part of a vehicle where the driver or passengers sit.

Carbon dioxide A gas found in the air, and used in fizzy drinks. It is made in some chemical reactions.

Chemical reaction A kind of change that can happen when different chemicals or substances mix together.

Corrugated cardboard Thick cardboard with a layer of folded rows of paper inside it to make it stronger, often used to make cardboard boxes.

Engineer Someone who designs, builds or maintains machines or structures, including vehicles and transport systems.

Expand To get bigger.

Glue gun A gun-shaped electric tool that heats up and applies strong glue.

Hoverboard A board with two wheels, used as a form of electric transport for one person.

Hub A place where passengers or goods can switch from one mode of transport to another.

Hull the body or frame of a ship, most of which goes under the water

Interchange Another word for a transport hub.

Leading edge The furthest forward edge of a propeller blade.

Maglev Short for magnetic levitation, a kind of train that hovers above its track using magnetic repulsion – a force that pushes two objects apart.

Paddle steamer A large boat that uses a steam-powered paddle or paddles to push it through the water.

Propeller A revolving set of angled blades, used on aircraft and boats to pull or push them forwards.

Repel To push away. Magnets can repel or attract each other.

Rotor blades The long narrow wings on top of a helicopter, which spin to give the helicopter lift.

Tailplane A small set of wings on the tail of an aircraft, which add lift and balance.

Tail rotor A small, vertical set of rotor blades on the tale of a helicopter, used to prevent the helicopter from turning when the main rotor blades spin.

Transit Another name for transport.

FURTHER INFORMATION

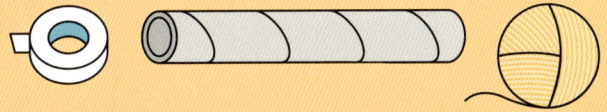

WHERE TO GET MATERIALS

Everyday items
You'll probably have some everyday items and craft materials at home already, such as pens and pencils, paper and card, string, sticky tape, glue, elastic bands and scissors.

Recycling
Old packaging that's going to be thrown away or recycled is a great source of making materials, such as cardboard boxes, plastic bottles, yoghurt pots, ice cream tubs, cardboard tubes, magazines, old wrapping paper and newspaper.

Supermarkets
Great for basic items you might not have at home, such as paper cups, straws, wooden skewers and chopsticks, vinegar and bicarbonate of soda.

Specialist shops
Hobby and craft shops, art shops, DIY stores and electronics shops are useful for things like a craft knife and a glue gun, paint, lolly sticks and magnets. If you don't have the shop you need near you, ask an adult to help you look for online shops such as Hobbycraft.

Charity shops
It's always a good idea to check charity shops when you can, as they often have all kinds of handy household items and craft materials at very low prices.

BOOKS

Paper Planes: Fold and Fly Amazing Planes! by Jenni Hairsine, Arcturus, 2019

Junk Re-Thunk by Brian Yanish, Henry Holt & Co., 2016

Science Makers: Making with Machines by Anna Claybourne, Wayland, 2018

Technical Tales: How to Build a Car by Martin Sodomka and Saskia Lacey, Walter Foster Jr., 2015

Junk Modelling by Annalees Lim, Wayland, 2016

WEBSITES

Fold 'N Fly
www.foldnfly.com
Dozens of paper plane designs to try, from easy to expert.

PBS Design Squad
pbskids.org/designsquad/
Lots of brilliant design and build challenges.

DIY
https://diy.org/
An online maker community for kids.

Parents.com Arts & Crafts
www.parents.com/fun/arts-crafts
Maker projects, instructions and videos.

Kiwico DIY page
www.kiwico.com/diy/
Fun and easy maker ideas.

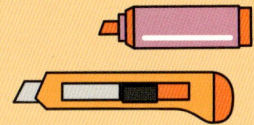

INDEX

A
axle 6, 7

B
boat 4, 8–9, 26, 29
bus 4, 7, 26

C
cabin 19, 21
cable car 10–11, 27, 28–29
car 4, 5–6, 26, 28–29
chemical reaction 23

E
elastic band 6, 7, 8, 9, 12, 14, 18, 20, 21
elastic band car 5–6, 28–29
elevator 16–17, 27, 28

F
flight 4, 12–15, 18–21, 22–23
float 4, 8

H
harbour 27, 29
helicopter 18–21, 29
helipad 26
hot air balloon 4
hover 4, 18, 25

J
jetpack 22–23, 28

L
landing skids 21
lift 16–17, 27, 28

M
maglev train 24–25, 26, 28
magnetic force 24, 25
magnetic levitation 24
magnets 24, 25

P
paddle 8, 9
paddle boat 8–9, 29
plane 4, 12–15, 26
platform 26, 27, 28
propeller 8, 12–15
propeller plane 12–15, 28

R
repel 24, 25
rotor blades 21

S
science 9, 15, 23, 24
station 27, 28
submarine 4

T
tail 15, 21
train 4, 24–25, 26, 27, 28
transport hub 26–27, 28–29

W
wheelchair 4
wheels 4, 7, 8
wings 15
Wright, Orville and Wilbur 12

MAKER MODELS

SERIES CONTENT LIST

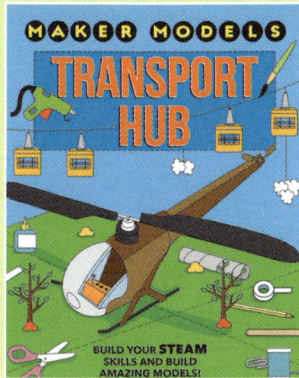

MAKER MODELS — TRANSPORT HUB
BUILD YOUR **STEAM** SKILLS AND BUILD AMAZING MODELS!

On the move! • Elastic band car • Paddle boat • Cable car • Propeller plane • Going up! • Helicopter • Jetpack • Maglev train • Multi-mode transport interchange • And here s your finished transport hub! • Glossary and further information • Index

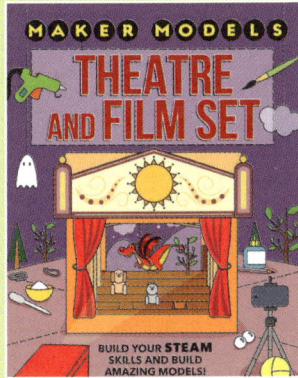

MAKER MODELS — THEATRE AND FILM SET
BUILD YOUR **STEAM** SKILLS AND BUILD AMAZING MODELS!

The stage is yours! • Theatre and stage • The swish of the curtain! • In the spotlight • Set design • Stars of the stage • Fly system • Gone in a puff of smoke • Pepper's ghost • Cinema projector • Stop-motion movie • Theatre house • And here's is your finished theatre! • Glossary and further information • Index

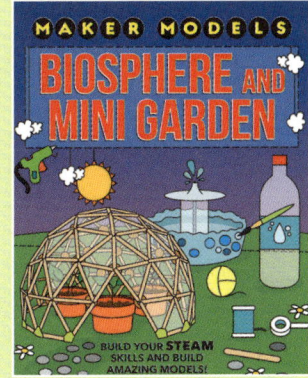

MAKER MODELS — BIOSPHERE AND MINI GARDEN
BUILD YOUR **STEAM** SKILLS AND BUILD AMAZING MODELS!

Grow a garden! • Garden base • Grass art • Bean tree • Wildflower corner • Geodesic dome greenhouse • Greenhouse garden • Fountain • Summer house • The finished garden • And here's is your finished biosphere and mini-garden! • Glossary and further information • Index

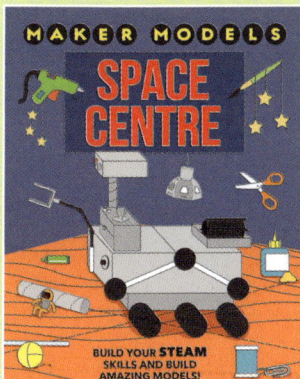

MAKER MODELS — SPACE CENTRE
BUILD YOUR **STEAM** SKILLS AND BUILD AMAZING MODELS!

Reach for the stars! • We have lift-off! • Launch pad • Command module • Parachute descent • Space satellite • Human gyroscope • Passenger spaceship • Mars rover • Planetarium projector • Space centre • And here is your finished space centre! • Glossary and further information • Index

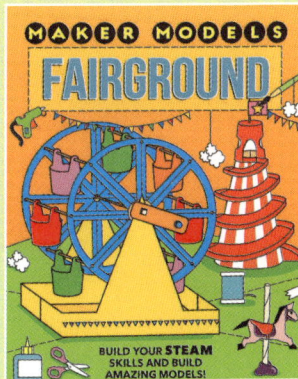

MAKER MODELS — FAIRGROUND

All the fun of the fair • Helter-skelter • Chair swing ride • Fairground stalls • Big wheel • Dodgems • Carousel • Rollercoaster • The fairground • Here is your finished fairground! • Glossary and further information • Index

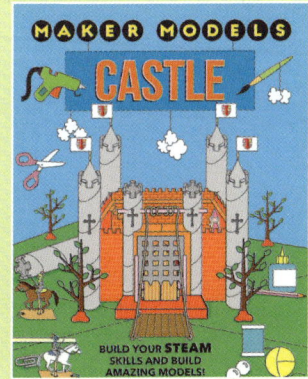

MAKER MODELS — CASTLE
BUILD YOUR **STEAM** SKILLS AND BUILD AMAZING MODELS!

Holding the fort • Castle walls and battlements • Towers and turrets • The grand gatehouse • Door and portcullis • Raise the drawbridge! • The great hall • The bedchamber • The secret room • The tilt yard • Mangonel attack! • The grounds and moat • And here is your fi nished castle! • Glossary and further information • Index

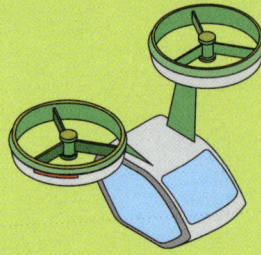

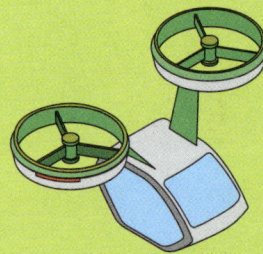